Arthur B. Stout

Chinese Immigration and the Physiological Causes of the

Decay of a Nation

Arthur B. Stout

Chinese Immigration and the Physiological Causes of the Decay of a Nation

ISBN/EAN: 9783337321451

Printed in Europe, USA, Canada, Australia, Japan

Cover: Foto ©Suzi / pixelio.de

More available books at **www.hansebooks.com**

CHINESE IMMIGRATION

AND

THE PHYSIOLOGICAL CAUSES

OF

THE DECAY OF A NATION.

BY ARTHUR B. STOUT, M. D.

San Francisco, 1862.

———————

SAN FRANCISCO:

AGNEW & DEFFEBACH, PRINTERS,

Corner Sansome and Merchant Streets.

1862.

CONTENTS.

PART I.

PART II;

IMPURITY OF RACE,

AS A

CAUSE OF DECAY.

PART I.

The Medical men disseminated through a state, are proper censors of the public health. It is their high province not only to cure disease, but to study and to promulgate the principles of Hygiene. In preventing the invasion of disease, they fulfill a more lofty, because more disinterested function, than in eradicating maladies already engendered. Occupying a high and influential position, their counsels and their teachings are all-powerful in contributing to improve the health, the strength, the vigor, both physical and intellectual, and also the endurance among nations of their race. It is in this view that I propose to examine the various causes which combine to deteriorate the American people.

I may at once state, in acknowledging my indebtedness, and in offering my humble tribute of gratitude to the high authorities whence I have drawn information, that I have freely consulted and drawn from the works of—

Brasseur de Bourbourg, Histoire des Nations Civilisées du Mexique et de l'Amérique Centrale durant les Siècles Antérieurs a Christophe Colomb.

Types of Mankind, Nott and Gliddon.

Volney, Ruines des Empires.

L'Abbé Huc, Journey Through China.

Morel, Dégénérescense de l'espéce humaine : Paris, 1857.

Combe, on the Constitution of Man.

Michelet, La Femme : 1860.

Davis' History of the Chinese.

Martin's History of China.

Gutzlaff's History of China.

The comprehensive work of Nott and Gliddon, replete with research, contains ample citations from Morton, Humboldt, Agassiz, and all the great authors upon the subject.

Sanger, History of Prostitution: 1859.

Claiming nothing original, but that the knowledge of science when once published is the property of mankind, I hope by adducing these high authorities to obtain more appreciation of my views than if presented on my own unaided responsibility. If the State of California can receive benefit from medical research, it is chiefly by drawing attention to the discoveries of modern science in the matters I shall treat of, and at the earliest moment in its history engrafting them upon her institutions.

Over the world is fast extending what is termed the great Caucasian Race of men. Children of migration, they move in vast waves over every continent. From the cradle to the grave they fluctuate in alternate ebb and flow over every region of Europe, vast tracts of Asia, the North and South of Africa, nearly all of North America, and are fast encroaching upon the South American continent. This is the race created with the highest endowments, and greatest aptitude under various circumstances, to encounter the vicissitudes of every clime and every soil. God speed it on its way!

One great division of this race, the Anglo-Saxon, is now occupying America, and the type thence arising is the one in which I am at present interested. The history of the rise and fall of empires sufficiently attests the migratory nature of the parent stock; and the American offspring appears abundantly imbued with the hereditary spirit.

In history, the brilliant details of wars and victories dazzle the sight and engross the mind. The student of history in witnessing the origin, the glory, and the demise of a nation, is apt to attribute to these wars, and their political sources, the catastrophe which he mourns. In searching among the ruins of the past to discover a guiding principle for the future, it is to these causes that he looks for his material.

But, in truth, a deeper cause, of which these wars and worldspread dissensions are only the effect, lies at the root of the evil. This cause. the ABUSE OF THE HUMAN SYSTEM, insidiously gnaws into each individual body, undermines the strength and beauty of God's noblest work, and thence penetrates, cancer-like, into the social, religious and political system. Thus contaminated, all the systems, in fatally allied conspiracy, attack the solidarity of the nation.

The originally predominant purity of the animal economy, and of the intellectual government, offer a short-lived resistance. Internal dissension, fostered by a consequently invited aggression, exhausts the power of the race, and a nation, vanquished by itself sinks into oblivion.

The action of the brain guides both the physical movements and the intellectual emanations. From the blood the brain derives its nutriment. If the aliment be rendered impure, the cerebral mechanism receives a corresponding alteration. As the blood degenerates so will the race of men ; and a degenerate nation can neither dictate to nor survive one of higher physical and intellectual endowment.

To the Caucasian race, with its varied types, has been assigned the supremacy in elevation of mind and beauty of form over all mankind. High over the rest it surveys the field of life. Appointed by the Creator to wield all human destinies, He has endowed it with the power above all others to study, to admire, and rule such of his Almighty works as enter within the sphere of man. No new combination of distinct existing races can improve this Divine excellence. Whatever enters it, tends to destroy it. In proportion to the rapidity with which deleterious elements are introduced, must be the ratio in the course of time of its degeneration and final extinction.

Our new American embranchment stands now isolated among nations in its purity and highest degree of cultivation and refinement, proudly rivaling them all. Yet, from the nature of its social and political institutions, more than all of them subject and exposed to a fearful pressure from without, it hence tends to destructive amalgamations, and the ruinous influences of conflicting political systems. These conditions are magnified by the mercenary efforts of self interest, by the abuse of a morbid philanthropy in liberal government, and by belief in the general equality of mankind.

The time to urge and impress the mind with the necessity of preserving the purity of race, is while the race is new, and thus close the door to amalgamations while the stock is pure and young. To permit the ingress of an inferior race is to strike at self-destruction. A government to protect its people should strive to preserve the purity of the race ; and, irrespective of political theories, should guard it from every amalgamation with inferior types.

No State of our Union is so exposed and threatened as California. At the very dawn of its existence it is menaced with the introduction of these pernicious elements ; and if now the struggle for life be not commenced, it must forever be abandoned. The degeneration will pursue its course, in personal and individual antipathies finding its only check.

I am led to these reflections from the contest now waging in regard to the Chinese immigration. It is stated that the Supreme Court has decided that the legislative statute preventive of this immigration is unconstitutional. But little versed in legal lore, I dare not oppose the wisdom of the Court in its constitutional decision. But, in a physiological view, the argument may yet be open. The first law of nature is to preserve the purity of the race—provided the race be of all others the superior. Self-preservation claims the first protective enactment. If the world mourns the presence of a Negro race in the Eastern and Southern States, what tears may be shed when, in the course of ages, the great West is overwhelmed with a Chinese immigration. Once permitted it must be forever endured. The work of degeneration once commenced, its progress must pursue its insidious and em-poisoning influence, not for a few years, but for centuries to come. The legislation now enacted is less for our own than for generations which, in the future, by their purity shall bless, or in their degeneration shall curse, their ancestral stock.

Among the causes I have yet to enumerate, which together combine to exhaust and degrade a race, the intermixture of blood with inferior races is the most potent and the most deplorable. All the arguments of the advantages of commerce, and the toleration of liberal government, sink into insignificance in comparison with the primary law of nature, which teaches self-preservation in protecting the purity of type in the race, and perpetuating the endurance of the nation. When we contemplate the ruins of empires, we read the neglect of these laws.

By the adoption of bad blood we voluntarily introduce the deadliest foe to our existence. If we but exclude this internal enemy, no outward force can crush our nation. It is in the healthful consolidation of all the means which invigorate the mental and physical energies, and the exclusion of all the constitutional destructive influences, that the highest type of mankind, all radiant with its manifold beauties, can be attained. All liberal laws are made special to the race which adopts them. There is no oppression in excluding inferior races from their enjoyment. By intermarrying with Europeans, we are but reproducing our own Caucasian type ; by commingling with the Eastern Asiatics, we are creating degenerate hybrids. We may seek to exchange commodities, but never to blend races. The argument that justice demands, while we are claiming free admission and intercourse with China, that we should freely open to the Chinese our portals and adopt them as our own, is not founded in nature. The Chinese may gladly court an American emigration to their land, for every combination improves and exalts their enervated race ; while, on the contrary, every permanent settlement of a Chinaman on our soil creates a depreciation in the blood of our own. " Commercial alliances, if you will, with all the nations upon the earth, but political alliances and social entanglements with none of them."

In thus refusing to the Eastern Asiatics the privilege of free immigration and permanent domicile in the land, I would not be thought to deny to an ancient and once enlightened race the merit due to their intelligence. Only it is vain for man to seek to unite that which the Creator has so distinctly divided. The Divine Will has imbued every race with excellent qualities, but has shown in the distinctions established in accordance with topography, clime and physological development, that they were not created to be indifferently blended.

In singular opposition to the freedom of admission of the Chinese, or "Indians," granted by the decision of the Supreme Court, stands their exclusion, by statute, from the privilege of giving testimony in court against one of the Caucasian race. This almost denies them the rights of human beings ; denies them the faculty to see, to hear, to tell the truth ; and with an arro-gance truly worthy of a " bamboo despotism," assumes a superi-ority far beyond the physiological differences of race which the Creator has designed. In Austria, a nobleman cannot be tried in a plebeian court. Our democratic country goes still further, and denies to both pure races, as well as hybrid modifications, the right to peril the life or property of a Caucasian. The law of the State declares the following persons shall not be witnesses :

" Indians, or persons having one-fourth or more of Indian blood. Negroes, or persons having one-half or more Negro blood."

In 1854, Judges Murray and Heydenfeldt, in rendering a judg-ment—The People v. Hall—state as follows :

" From that time," the landing of Columbus in America, " the American Indians, and the Mongolian or Asiatic were regarded as the same type of the human species."

" At the period whence the legislation dates, those portions of Asia which include India proper, the Eastern Archipelago, and the countries washed by the Chinese waters, were denominated the Indies, from which the inhabitants had derived the generic name of Indians."

"Ethnology at that time was unknown as a distinct science, or if known, had not reached that high point of perfection which it has since attained by the scientific inquiries and discoveries of the master minds of the last half century. Few speculations had been made with regard to the moral or physical differences be-tween the different races of mankind."

The learned Judges, then, with much apparent reluctance, admit and say : " Although the discoveries of eminent archeolo-gists and the researches of modern geologists have given to this continent an antiquity of thousands of years anterior to the evi-dence of man's existence, and the light of modern science may have shown conclusively that it was *not* peopled by the inhabi-tants of Asia, but that the Aborigines are a distinct type, and as such claim a distinct origin ; still, this would not alter the meaning of the term (Indian), and render that specific which was before generic."

We have then two races of Indians, the Asiatic or Mongolian, and the American Indians, the Aborigines of the continent. The American Aborigines are only termed Indians because the original discoverers of America supposed they had reached the Indies by a western route when they arrived at the West India Islands. Both are pure blood races, and both possess their peculiar and eminent qualities. Although experience proves they cannot blend as races with the Caucasian, without detriment to the last race, yet it has never shown that they are unworthy of respect and honor in their rank among nations.

Who can regard the magnificent monuments of China, the excellence of her arts, the extent of her productions, and the refinement of her parental government before the Tartar dynasty, and say a Chinaman dare not open his lips in testimony for or against a white man? Who can contemplate the vast ruins of Central America, whose splendor still defies the wreck of time, the mounds of the United States, the traces everywhere of former power and thought, and refuse to the Aboriginal of America, fallen as he may be, the right to confront the aggressive Caucasian in the cause of justice? We may hold the Negro our slave, but as nature has created him with sufficient qualities to render him of value, even as a slave, he should still be allowed to see, to hear, and tell the truth. The mixed races, in their turn, should have their testimony taken at its value ; but yet, though freely associated with at one moment, they are turned out of court the next. Thus, in supercilious pride, the white lord disdains the laws of nature ; and while he too often converts them to his purposes, subverts the natural claims of God's creatures. These are the tyrannies which in time combine to overthrow his empire. If individual worthlessness cancel the value of a testimony let it be rejected as individual, but deny not to races their innate prerogatives. The same law which would restore their natural right would guard against its abuse. False testimony may be given in either case ; we avoid its liability by statutory provisions. A radical principle should not be denied because errors of fact may endanger its application.

In ages far remote, when the historian shall search the records of the past, it will be in the laws of the State, as its best and most authentic monuments, that he will estimate the degree of civilization to which the people had attained. Laws, then, should immediately follow in the wake of science. They should be modified with the progressive knowledge of the day. We contend these laws are not the index of the age, nor do they express our degree of civilization. They may have suited the era of Columbus, but science in ethnology, geology and archeology has doomed to forgetfulness those old ideas.

A broadcast view over the country will show the progress of deterioration by the blending of races, as it insidiously but surely advances.

To illustrate the ramifications which result from the fusion of three races—the Caucasian, the Aboriginal American, and the Negro—I take the arrangement of Tschudi, and adopted by Nott and Gliddon :

PARENTS.	CHILDREN.
White father and Negro mother	Mulatto.
" " and Indian mother	Mestiza.
Indian father and Negro mother	Chino.
White father and Mulatto mother	Cuarteron.
" " and Mestiza mother	Creole, pale brownish complexion.
" " and Chino mother	Chino-blanco.
" " and Cuarterona mother	Quintero.
" " and Quintera mother	White.
Negro father and Indian mother	Zambo.
" " and Mulatto mother	Zambo-negro.
" " and Mestiza mother	Mulatto-oscuro.
" " and Chino mother	Zambo-chino.
" " and Zamba mother	Zambo-negro, perfectly black.
" " and Quintera mother	Mulatto, rather dark.
Indian father and Mulatto mother	Chino-oscuro.
" " and Mestiza mother	Mestizo-claro, frequently very beautiful·
" " Chino mother	Chino-cola.
" " and Zamba mother	Zambo-claro.
" " and Chino-Chola mother	Indian, with frizzly hair.
" " and Quintera mother	Mestizo, rather brown.
Mulatto father and Zamba mother	Zambo, a miserable race.
" " and Mestiza mother	Chino, rather clear complexion.
" " and Chino mother	Chino, rather dark.

Here, then, are twenty-three varieties, or crosses, occupying our soil with their progeny, and multiplying their kind, to the continual detriment of the Caucasian race. "To define their characteristics correctly," adds the learned German, " would be impossible, for their minds partake of the mixture of their blood. As a general rule, it may be fairly said, that they unite in themselves all the faults, without any of the virtues, of their progenitors ; as men they are generally inferior to the pure races, and as members of society they are the worst class of citizens."

On some of these mixtures the author is doubtless too severe, for several of them possess commendable qualities, but are always far inferior to the pure white race. It will be seen that Tschudi gives the scientific definition of the term Creole. This does not regard the signification indulgently given to the term in some of the Southern States, where it is simply applied to the native offspring of foreign parents, even when the parentage is pure white. The author studied these amalgations in Peru ; but in the United States, where more benign institutions exist, their better qualities being elicited, and their vices repressed, they appear in a more favorable aspect. These combinations, to the number of many millions, are now engrafting themselves, with their injurious tendencies, upon our race. Their increase is immense. However impossible or inexpedient it may be to disturb them, is a question of national policy, as "better to bear the ills we have, than fly to those we know not of." Still, in the pro- gress of ages the pernicious element cannot fail to augment, and greatly to the detriment of the pure and superior race.

Let us now in imagination pass over a space of two hundred years, and observe the country when, in addition to the American Indian and Negro amalgamation, the Asiatic Indian shall have had free scope ; when, in that time which for nationalities is short, the Chinese, Japanese, Malays and Mongolians of every caste, shall have overrun the land ; when they, in their turn, have given origin to their countless varieties of hybrid creatures. As the locusts of California overrun the fields of the husbandman, will these swarms of beings degenerate our land. In the progress of this debasing alloy, and in the course of time, may another Vol- ney follow his guiding genius from " those ramparts of Ninevah, those walls of Babylon, those palaces of Persepolis, those temples of Balbeck and of Jerusalem," and after dwelling a time in mournful meditation over those yet more ancient forest-covered ruins of Mexico and Central America, come to pour out his last lamentations on the crumbling remains of our own Republic.

THE REMEDY.

What is the remedy for this vast evil? Early prevention is the only specific. Plant not the germs and there will be naught to eradicate. While the Chinese immigration is controlled by a few leading men, heads of societies, or Hong merchants, its restriction may be easily accomplished. The correction must commence at its source. Better would it be for our country that the hordes of Genghis Khan should overflow the land, and with armed hostility devastate our vallies with the sabre and the fire-brand than that these more pernicious hosts, in the garb of friends, should insidiously poison the well-springs of life, and spreading far and wide, gradually undermine and corrode the vitals of our strength and prosperity. In the former instance we might oppose the invasion with sword and rifled cannon; but this destructive intrusion enters by invisible approaches—is aided and fostered in its advance by those who forget or never dream of their country's interest, while they seek to advance their private ends.

When the engrafting is thus perfected, eradication becomes impossible. Let the Attilas of Asiatic despotism appear, and every freeman will prove to be a Meroveg; but against a Coolie who can struggle? What though the labor of Coolies be cheaper than that of the stalwart men of our own race? We must nevertheless lose by the exchange. If the former drive back these hardy pioneers, who shall defend the land? Who shall whiten the plains with their homesteads? Who shall form the families of the Republic? The vigorous strength of Caucasian labor cannot be nourished with a handful of rice, nor will their intelligence for their own emolument, or their aspirations for their children, accept existence in a state of protracted Coolieism or serfdom. Reduce their wages to the rates of Coolieism and you degrade them, physically and morally, to the state of Coolies.

Our native and adopted people require the higher rates of wages, for they have higher functions than mere daily labor to perform. They are the volunteers in the promotion and the defence of the rights of man. To them we look for the maintenance of the Union and the progress of civilization. If, by inadequate recompense for their labor, we banish them eastward from our frontier and adopt the Chinese immigrant in their stead, who will repel the foreign aggressor whom war shall invite to our shore? What part in the fierce drama of national defence will the Coolie play? Why, exactly the part of the crow in an unguarded cornfield—to sieze the grain and fly at the first sign of gunpowder.

The preventive remedies are :

I. The action of the General Government to reform our treaty stipulations with the Empire of the East.

II. The intervention of the Legislature of the State to enact such laws as shall be radical in preventing immigration.

III. The encouragement of local associations to elevate every possible barrier to its progress.

IV. The cultivation of a public opinion which shall be all powerful to discountenance the employment of Chinese labor. It is not my province to enter into the details of these four classes of remedial agents. I leave them to the more competent authorities in their respective departments, and respectfully invite all to co-operate therein, from the Executive at Washington to the humblest operative whose voice speaks by a ballot.

It is appropriate to ask, what is the position which the Asiatic stranger should receive in the State? What national view should be taken of his desire to visit the country? In what aspect should he appear to every generous citizen? The just reply would be, he should be regarded as a guest in a foreign land. "Stranger is a holy name." The munificent host should extend to him his cheerful and enriching hospitality. It may not always be requited here, but our adventurers on Asiatic soil may receive the reward. With the extension of commerce and the increase of associations which thence arise with this remarkable nation, the fairest facilities for the agents of both parties, and respectively in each other's country, should be encouraged. My argu. ments against extended immigration, permanent residence or adoption as freeholders, are entirely distinct from these commercial considerations.

I do not seek to embarrass trade, but I do desire to prohibit immigration as a national measure to obtain population; to dispose of public or private lands; to acquire cheap labor, or to consult the convenience of reckless speculators. Let us receive the Chinaman, whether Mandarin or Coolie, with a respect due to his ancient grandeur, his still existing power and ability. Let us refuse him permanent domicile, elective rights, title in fee to land, declare null by statute intermarriage, and compel the ultimate return of every trader to his native land. With a con. stantly increasing commerce his total exclusion is impracticable. Let us, therefore, receive him as a transient resident, teach him our language, inspire him with regard for our religion, instru^{..}- him in the principles of our sciences, initiate him into the deta^{ils} of all our practical arts, display to him our improved engine^{es}, manufacturing machinery, improved implements of trade, and o^{ur} economical modes of labor-saving husbandry.

Let us imbue him with a love of all the refinements of o^{ur} social system, and a desire to adopt the extended comforts of o^{ur} mode of living. Let Chinamen thus accomplished return to the^{ir} native homes, and diffuse, broad-spread, the instruction thus a^{c-} quired.

These are the influences which convert a nation. This is pra^{c-} tical Christianity : this is the means to protect the purity of o^{ur} own race, and elevate the other to the highest degree of attai^{na-} ble civilization. The history of China gives the most convinci^{ng} testimony that the Chinese people, in earlier ages, received wth welcome, and were exceedingly disposed universally to ad^{pt} the Christian religion. Its missionaries, pious, fervent an^d devoted as individuals, were honored for their scientific attair ments. Their knowledge in mathematics and astronomy pro moted them to the highest places of preferment.

Emperors themselves were softened by their influence an[.] yielded to their persuasion. Their Christian doctrine receive[.] a wide extension, and Christian altars arose among heathe temples. But it soon appeared that to accept the Christian worshi[.] it would be necessary to submit to Roman rule. The adoption ^f Christian rites involved the disintegration of political structure[.] To save the Empire they must reject the new religion. T^e snow white robes of the Church concealed in their folds the ke^s of Empire and an iron sceptre. To escape the latter they r[.] jected the whole. As they had surrounded themselves with [.]

material wall to exclude the inimical Tartars, so they enveloped themselves in political exclusion to evade revolutionizing doctrine. Christianity was not offered to them as a heaven-sent boon without a price. Its intrinsic worth and beauty was to cost Empire and independence ; to be harvested in subjection and be mulcted by tyranny.

The Christianity we offer is for its own enlightenment. We ask no sway ; we seek no territory. The seeds we plant offer their ten-fold harvest for the benefit alone of the nation which reaps.

The anti-Christian religions of Asia should constitute an insurmountable bar to the free admission of Asiatics on this continent. While but few are here, the occasional appearance of an idol temple may not be of consequence ; but when, ere long, the immigration, if not prevented, will be immense, these people will claim permission to worship according to their Oriental doctrine.

In every valley and over every plain Christian churches and heathen temples, side by side, will offer their grotesque contrast to the sight. It may be safely questioned whether, in admitting into our Constitution the free toleration of all religions, the framers of our Magna Charta had any other than Christian doctrines in their view. Their attention was engrossed with the European systems and the controversies from which they had just escaped. Had they foreseen the extension of territory which their young Republic was destined to acquire, and the close intercourse with the Asiatic world which would ensue, they would have confined within Christian limits such universal toleration.

The population of China exceeds 300,000,000 of inhabitants. The territory they occupy is scarcely large enough to contain them. Although the aggregate amount of their labor is immense, the great majority of them can only obtain a scanty subsistence by the most patient and incessant industry. Extreme poverty universally prevails, and a recompense inconceivably small is the reward of their toil. Hundreds of thousands of these impoverished beings would gladly escape to other realms if the opportunity were offered them to improve their condition. The overflow from their native land to this country, if no restriction withheld them, would be immense, and the Vanderbilts of com-

2

merce would even now have covered the seas with their fleets if no barrier intervened to prevent their transportation to our State. We owe to their own laws and to the peculiar tenets of their religion our immunity from this inundation. The very limited number of Chinese which, under special contracts, are permitted to emigrate are compelled by law to return within a specified time, or, in case of death, the rites of their religion require that their remains be restored for interment in their ancestral graveyards.

Thus are we indebted to foreign laws and not to our own precautions for the salvation of the country.

Let but these barriers burst and we have no protection from the hosts which will flow across the Pacific. That these barriers will burst is the manifest destiny of the Chinese nation. The most casual observer must easily discern that an entire social, religious, and political reorganization is in progress throughout the whole of Asia. This metamorphosis is her infallible destiny. If Asia is to participate in the refinements of civilization and the progress of human culture throughout the world, she must accede to and adopt this radical revolution. With or without her consent this destiny will be accomplished. Time is the only question. The encroachments of English power from the west, the gradual but certain approaches of Russia from the north, the allied fleets of England and of France which hover along and seek admission by her eastern shores, must eventually overwhelm the Asiatic continent. India crushed by the grasping hand of trade; the Hindoos brutalized in their idolatry; and China torn by rebellion, poisoned with opium and starving in poverty, must fall together in one general ruin. Railroads and canals will penetrate the deserts; the lightning telegrams which will shortly flash through the Russian Empire of the North, and the navies armed with all the batteries of modern invention, which invest the continent, all concentrate their intellectual and physical resources against the numerous but defenceless nations of Asia If England and France, for their own aggrandizement, arrested for a while the encroaching power of the Czar at Sebastopol they gave to Oriental exclusiveness its death blow at Pekin

The former act can have but limited effect, but the second will be forever permanent.

Thus do all civilized nations, while advancing their varied interests, combine to destroy the ancient religions and idolatries of Asia, and regenerate its exhausted races. Islamism and Paganism must alike sink into oblivion, and Christianity enter, like sunlight into chaos, to illuminate and revivify this ancient world. Be it so ; and when this destiny shall be accomplished will be the moment to review our national policy, repeal preventive laws and admit Asiatics to the privileges of freemen.

PART II.

I have now to consider other causes which singly, or in combination, when acting upon the human system, impede its normal
development or undermine and enervate its beauty and strength.
Of these, are first, hereditary diseases, as phthisis or consumption, scrofula, syphilis, mental alienation, and epidemic diseases :
secondly, material agents deleterious to the human economy. The
first class acts in a double manner on the individuals themselves
subject to the maladies, and secondarily on their progeny. The
second class, comprising active material agents used to excess,
contains all the stimulant as well as the narcotic agents resorted
to by man to exalt his enjoyments or appease his miseries. They
are opium, tobacco, fermented liquors, and all stimulo-narcotic
agents more or less in common use as luxuries of life.

It will readily be perceived that each one of these causes is
worthy of a monograph ; but the present occasion compels me to
group them, and sweep over the field with hasty speed.

Could I in one terse page exhibit all the miseries, all the degradation, all the ruin which the abuse of these agents has, in the
great revolution of time, accumulated upon the human races, not
all the famed artists of the past, nor the ambitious aspirants to
future greatness, would suffice to portray the dreadful picture.
Could I annihilate them, the arsenal of death would be well
nigh exhausted.

As the maladies indicated in the first class are in many cases
only the effect of the agents enumerated in the second class, the
above arrangement is not arbitrary, but for convenience alone.

PHTHISIS AND SCROFULA.

Phthisis, or Consumption, and Scrofula are, of all others, the
most destructive maladies of our country. To expatiate upon
their insidious invasion, enumerate their manifold manifestations

describe the fear and anxiety which invests their suspected existence, or enter into their minute pathology, is foreign to my subject. To evoke their causes, and indicate the mode to evade
their intrusion upon the animal economy, is a matter of public
hygiene. The individual who once so lives as to engender in his
system the germ of these diseases, commits an enduring wrong
upon his lineal successors. These diseases, in their chronic or
hereditary condition, are diseases of debility, and entail upon the
families they invade a successively enfeebling progeny. For the
climatic influences which lay their foundation, men can scarcely
be responsible, except in the careless neglect of the sanitary
measures which protect the system from changes of weather.
But other causes combine to give them origin. These are, the
gradual but long-continued introduction into the economy of
agents which for a time stimulate, yet ultimately enervate
its powers, and radically alter the constituents of the animal
tissues.

When a rich, healthful, normal blood no longer permeates the
blood vessels, distributing to the various tissues their quota of
natural components, and when the brain no longer daily
receives its adequate allowance of pure blood, its reflex influences
upon the tissues are correspondingly altered and necessarily
vitiated. Degeneration, with its series of hereditary contam-
inations of the pure type, commences. Thence may be traced
the origin, in numerous instances, of miliary tubercles, whether
of the lungs, brain or bones, and the enervation of scrofulosis.

SYPHILIS.

Who can calculate the innumerable losses to society and its
population which result from neglected Syphilis! Its deeply
engrafted poison follows in the race to every generation, except
in those instances where its immediate or hereditary presence
produces sterility, and then the State loses a family.

How often are the best directed efforts of science in curing
uterine maladies and restoring fertility, rendered ineffectual!
The latent virus has stricken its victim, and too often, even when
suspected or detected, refuses to relax its grasp. The influence
of this malady upon the uterus is either entirely to arrest development, to degenerate its product, or to produce the actual death

of the ovum. Fortunate for society, except in a numerical point of view, when the arrest of development or the death of the progeny occurs—for its elaboration is always defective, and a race of a lower type produced.

MENTAL ALIENATION.

I must touch for a moment the vast subject of Mental Aliena-tion. When the empire of the brain over the economy is once profoundly injured and subverted, all that long train of heart-rending diseases which fill the asylums devoted to insanity is founded. The perverted mind and distorted body are together the dreadful signs of the degradation which ensues from the abuse of the laws of nature, and excess in the use of the agents given to man for enjoyment and the perpetuation of his perfect race. This subject opens to view the great national question of alcoholic intoxication, or the empoisonment of the system by the abuse of fermented liquors. Its exponents fill our hospitals, alms-houses, orphan asylums, lunatic asylums and prisons. With-out attempting to advert to all the maladies which arise from this cause, or dilate upon idiocy, mania, epilepsy, delirum tremens, softening of the brain. hereditary mania, atrophy of general form and strength, paralysis. and general depravation, both moral and physical, of the system, I shall draw upon Morel for a picture of the condition of Sweden, and ask every reader, from the deplo-rable condition of another country, to draw the natural deduction for our own, and from their fate learn our own salvation :

"There are annually manufactured in Sweden, on the most moderate calculation, 2,000,000 litres of brandy of the country. But very little of this is exported. Sweden contains 3,000.000 inhabitants. By deducting from this number the children, a large number of women, and persons whose local position forces them to moderation, 1,500,000 inhabitants remain who annually con-sume each from eighty to one hundred litres of brandy. It is easy to perceive the progressive decay in those families in which the alcoholic degeneration has controlled the mass of the hered-itary phenomena."

"It is an indisputable fact," says Huss, a scientific Swede, "that the Swedish people in their stature and their physical force have degenerated from their ancestry." Translating again from Morel, he states that "it is certain that the constitution of the Swedes has undergone considerable pathological modifications. It is vain to seek in the country those men of the North so boasted of by historians and poets." Special maladies, as chronic gastritis and scrofula, have, in frightful extension, become general. An affection, formerly unknown—Chlorosis—has invaded all classes, as well rich as poor, and rages both through the country and in the cities.

Into this state of health, the details of which I omit, other causes may indeed enter ; but alcoholism, with its persistent but degenerating erythism, enters for a very large proportion. No person of experience will deny the indispensable necessity of the use of fermented liquors under circumstances of unusual fatigue of mind or body, nor their importance as a remedial agent in adynamic diseases. Their moderate use to enhance the enjoyments of the festal hour, has been admitted for all time. It is their steady, persistent abuse until the blood has become vitiated —until the brain no longer performs its normal functions—until the constituent solid tissues of the body are involved in the disease, and the mental erythism of alcohol combines with corresponding enervation of body to destroy the healthy structure, impoverish the body and degenerate the progeny, that they are to be inveighed against as poisons. It is then they create their hereditary maladies ; it is then the vice of the parent is perpetuated in the offspring, ruins the family and degenerates the nation. Who has not seen in the features of the child the altered likeness of the inebriate father ? To illustrate these varied conditions, the plates of Morel will serve better than elaborate phrases, and to them I refer the reader. Thus it is that the sins of the parents are visited on their children "unto the third and fourth generations."

TOBACCO.

The consumption of tobacco is increasing annually to an enormous amount. In intensity of action upon the system, it excels the different stimulo-narcotic agents used in other countries. It surpasses hasheesh and opium in activity if taken internally, and stands prominent as a deleterious agent, when abused, to the vigor and health of the economy. If our Government require funds for war, let taxation fall heaviest on these articles ; then, at least, may the consumer, while he ruins himself, enrich the nation. It would be interesting to trace its enervating influence in its varied symptoms, but a recapitulation of the deleterious effects of all this class of substances may be found in the consequences of the abuse of opium, as narrated by authors who have studied it among a people addicted to its excessive abuse.

OPIUM.

The Abbé Huc states, that " at present China purchases opium annually of the English to the amount of £35,000,000. Large fine vessels, armed like ships of war, serve as depots to the English merchants. These rich speculators live habitually in the midst of gaiety and splendor, and think little of the frightful consequences of their detestable traffic. When from their superb palace-like mansions on the seashore, they see their beautiful vessels returning from the Indies, gliding majestically over the waves, and entering with all sails spread into the port, they do not reflect that the cargoes borne in these superb clippers are bringing ruin and desolation to numbers of families. With the exception of some rare smokers, who, thanks to a quite exceptional organization ! are able to restrain themselves within the bounds of moderation, all others advance rapidly toward death, after having passed through the successive stages of idleness, debauchery, poverty, the ruin of their physical strength, and the complete prostration of their intellectual and moral faculties. Nothing can stop a smoker who has made much progress in this habit ; incapable of attending to any kind of business, insensible to every event, the most hideous poverty and the sight of a family plunged into despair and misery cannot rouse him to the smallest exertion, so complete is the disgusting apathy in which he is sunk."

The use of opium, to an abuse, and as a deleterious stimulant, is becoming more and more familiar to Americans, but the vice bears no comparison to that of China. The moment to cure the disease is, however, to strike it in its infancy. With the fearful picture, then, of the destructive influence on the system of the abuse of opium in China, why should not a legal enactment restrain the sale of the fatal drug?

THE REMEDY.

What barrier can be placed to the invasion and progress of these ruinous causes of degeneration? Several I have already proposed. The most important, however, consists in intellectual, moral and physical education. The secret of public health and national endurance is in the promotion of public instruction. Our political and social organization is now the reverse of that of ancient times. Then education and power were allied in the Imperial Court; and as in that was associated the idea of the God-head, it comprised the unbounded influence of religious faith. The chief of the nation was its divinity, and all laws for the happiness of the people founded on justice, and consolidated by idolatry, emanated from the throne. While the throne remained pure in principle and virtuous in act, the nation governed progressed in enlightenment, flourished in its institutions and population, was influential in peace and invincible in war. Its world-renowned monuments, the admiration of every age, attest the riches and grandeur of such states. The moment corruption and licentiousness penetrated the palace, the nobility caught the rapid contagion. They quickly contaminated the public mind, and from that hour commenced the ruin and downfall of the nation. In our own Republic the wisdom of the public councils reflects only the knowledge of the people. As they are instructed in virtue and science will they select the representatives of their mind in Senates and Assemblies. From degenerate and ignorant sources cannot emanate the lofty principles and excellent laws which win the admiration of rival powers, and perpetuate the nation. Hence it is in the deficiency of education, which should be all-pervading, that may be found the incessant routine of inoperative laws, unconstitutional enactments, time-wasting appeals and decisions reversed. The greatest feature in the art of creating an enduring nation is in the radical education of its youth. Where and how shall this cultivation of youth commence? It is in the education of women. The matrons of a state form its heroes. Therefore should the cultivation of women embrace not only beautiful and graceful accomplishments, but substantial education, the acquirement of physiological instruction, and the care of the physical development of the form.

The vigorous constitution begets the energetic mind. To quote a recent writer : " Specially should females be taught the responsible duties of maternity, in order that a race of better developed beings may bless the world ; one of fewer excesses ; one of more harmoniously developed natures ; one of more healthy progenitive or hereditary influence. When women are thus taught, no fear need be had for the youth." Says Michelet : " *Woman is an altar*, a pure and holy one, to which man, shattered by the vicissitudes of life, repairs, day by day, to renew his faith, and restore his faltering conscience. preserved more pure in her than in him. *Woman is a school*, from whom truly generations receive their belief. Long before the father dreams of education the mother has profoundly implanted her own, which can never be effaced." In the cause of public instruction a state cannot appropriate its funds with too great liberality. There is more economy in founding institutions of public instruction than in building prisons and houses of refuge. Their growth decreases the never-ending expenditures on hospitals, asylums and alms-houses. Prominent in all education should be that of the physical development. Especially is the remark applicable to that of females. The institutions devoted to their instruction are neglectful of the appliances to improve their physical strength and health. Pre-occupied in the rivalry of precocious minds, they forget that all their success is compromised by neglect of physical health and vigor. Great precocity in youth is seldom followed by healthful old age. It is in the well proportioned development of both body and mind that the true progress of the people may be discerned.

The health, vigor and beauty of the rising race of California's children might make these observations appear unnecessary. In San Francisco at least 10,000 youth, the fairest of Heaven's creation, appear to prove the favorable auspices under which we live. The same ratio prevails throughout the State. To foster, improve and exalt these by every care in mental and physical development, by every legislative enactment thereto conducive and by any expenditure which can promote the object, is a worthy labor. If in my views I have taken a wide range, it is because the interest of our State has an equivalent magnitude ; for the conservation of our race comprises centuries in its limits.

www.ingramcontent.com/pod-product-compliance
Lightning Source LLC
Chambersburg PA
CBHW021551270326
41930CB00008B/1458